Original title:
The Ivy Chronicles

Copyright © 2025 Creative Arts Management OÜ
All rights reserved.

Author: Victor Mercer
ISBN HARDBACK: 978-1-80581-747-5
ISBN PAPERBACK: 978-1-80581-274-6
ISBN EBOOK: 978-1-80581-747-5

Vinebound Wishes

A creeping vine with dreams so bright,
It whispers tales to the moon at night.
Beneath its leaves, the laughter flows,
With every twist, new silly shows.

A flower sneezes, pollen flies,
Mimicking the buzzing flies.
Snails in capes slide down the wall,
In a garden race, they have a ball.

The Collected Starlight

Stars dropped down to tickle toes,
Dancing on the earth like prose.
With jars in hand, we catch their light,
Laughing as they take their flight.

Crickets sing in tuneful jest,
Each note a giggle, nature's best.
In the glow of laughter's spree,
We find the magic, wild and free.

Leafy Memories of Old

Once there lived a leafy sage,
Who turned each frown into a page.
With tiny hats, the leaves would wear,
In leafy gossip, they'd all share.

The apples danced to a silly tune,
While pumpkins grooved beneath the moon.
They formed a band of veggie cheer,
With every joke, they spread good cheer.

Threads of Nature's Tapestry

In a quilt made of threads so fine,
Woven tales of grape and vine.
With squirrels stitching puffs of fun,
They craft a patchwork for everyone.

A rabbit hops on a sunny patch,
Telling stories with a playful scratch.
Nature giggles, it can't resist,
In the colorful threads, it finds its bliss.

Nature's Veiled Storyteller

Beneath the leaves, secrets hide,
The whispers of trees, oh what a ride!
Squirrels gossip, birds in a cheer,
Nature's tales that tickle the ear.

Mossy carpets chuckle and sigh,
As mushrooms dance, oh me, oh my!
A cheeky breeze steals hats from heads,
Leaves rustle jokes, no tears or dreads.

Journey through Verdant Paths

Hopping along on emerald trails,
Where every corner tells wild tales.
A frog in a tux, ready to sing,
And rabbits plotting their next big fling.

The sun peeks out, a playful tease,
Dancing shadows, a gentle breeze.
Lost in laughter, we tumble and roll,
Nature's humor warms the soul.

Vines that Bind and Blossom

Around the trees, they twist and twirl,
Vines gossip like best friends in a whirl.
Tickling the barks in a playful spree,
With blooms that laugh, wild and free.

A bee in a bowtie sips sweet wine,
While ladybugs break out the sunshine.
They gather 'round for a party so grand,
With petals and pollen, it's quite the band!

Chronicles of the Forest's Breath

In the shade where the mischief stays,
Whimsical winds weave through the maze.
Trees dance along in silly pairs,
With stories to share, like old goofy bears.

Bats in sunglasses hold a soirée,
While owls hoot jokes that never decay.
The forest chuckles, a secret delight,
As night falls softly, bathed in moonlight.

The Confluence of Life and Leaf

In a garden so wild, where the humor has bloomed,
Lived a vine with a plan, or so it presumed.
It tangled with flowers, quite bold and so brash,
Who knew that a leaf could create such a clash?

The daisies complained, they felt quite confined,
While the roses just laughed, thinking nature's unkind.
The ivy just giggled, with mischief in tow,
Wrapped round all the petals, causing quite the show!

A bumblebee buzzed, with a grin on its face,
"Why so serious, vines? You're just part of the race!"
With a flick of a leaf, the show took a turn,
Even weeds joined the dance, oh how they would churn!

In this confluence, chaos treated with flair,
Nature's great comedy, no moment to spare.
So when you pass by, give a wink and a cheer,
For the life and the leaf all conspire here!

Beneath the Canopy of Time

Beneath leaves that wiggle and sway,
Lies a secret garden where squirrels play.
Whispers of laughs, echoes so bright,
Even the gnomes are lost in delight.

One time a bird tried to learn to dance,
Twisting around like it had lost its chance.
It tripped on a twig, fell flat on its face,
Now it just hops with a whole lot of grace.

Tendrils of Memory

They say the vines know all the tales,
Of muddy boots and comical fails.
There's a story about a cat named Lou,
Who got tangled up, not a clue what to do.

With each twist and turn of a growing vine,
Laughter bubbles up, so joyfully fine.
It's pure mayhem, this garden of cheer,
Where flowers tell jokes, we all want to hear.

The Veil of Verdant Recollections

In a leafy nook where time takes a break,
Old lady bugs giggle as they bake.
With dough made of pollen and sunshine too,
They invite every bug for a buttery chew.

A butterfly flutters with a hat on its head,
Said it was 'Fashion Week' without being fed.
Fashionably late, it trips on a petal,
And ends up in the jam with a terrible meddle.

Embracing the Wild

Branches sway with a whimsical tune,
As a raccoon prances beneath the moon.
He's got a top hat and a cane made of wood,
Dancing like nobody else ever could.

Daisies giggle as the moonlight shines,
While worms discuss where to draw the lines.
A frog joins in, hops to the beat,
Claiming he's the world's best dancer on feet.

Heartbeats among the Foliage

In the garden, a squirrel skids,
Dancing like a kid with a hundred bids.
Leaves whisper secrets as they sway,
While bugs plan parties for the day.

Bees zoom in like buzzing cars,
Daffodils twist, trying to be stars.
The sun's a jester, casting bright rays,
While nature laughs through leafy haze.

Rabbits play hopscotch, oh what a sight,
Chasing shadows in the fading light.
Worms groove to tunes only they hear,
In the foliage where hearts lose their fear.

So here we are, among the greens,
Where laughter echoes, and bliss convenes.
With every heartbeat in the air,
Nature spins tales that prompt us to care.

The Symphony of Silent Growth

In a corner of the garden, quiet tunes,
Earthworms sway beneath the silver moon.
Flowers gossip, petals in a twist,
Tickling the ferns, who can't resist.

Moss grows softer than a purring cat,
While snails slow-dance with a minor spat.
Raindrops tap dance, a joyful sound,
As roots plot mischief beneath the ground.

Trees applaud with rustling leaves,
Sharing jokes that only they believe.
The grass embellishes the plot with flair,
While crickets chirp their witty snare.

Among this symphony, laughter brews,
Where even the thorns can't help but muse.
Each hidden corner tells a funny tale,
A world of wonder where giggles prevail.

Lush Elegies of the Woods

Under the canopy, secrets are spun,
Where mushrooms gather to sing and run.
Fallen leaves cheer with a crackle and pop,
While a chubby raccoon does a silly hop.

The brook giggles, splashing away,
Tickled by stones that join in the play.
Squirrels debate who's the best acorn thief,
While hedgehogs roll with unending grief.

Foxes play hide-and-seek in the grove,
In a game only they seem to solve.
Whispers of laughter ripple through the air,
While the sun's golden crown gives us flair.

Thus, in this lush realm, we softly sigh,
With chuckles that echo, oh how they fly!
For in the woods, life's quirks hold sway,
In every rustle, there's fun at play.

Vines and Verities

Vines twist tales on the garden wall,
Spilling secrets with giddy enthrall.
Caterpillars stretch with a quirky grace,
While dandelions puff in wild embrace.

Frog orchestras croak with pure delight,
As twinkling fireflies dance in the night.
A cactus grins, proud of its spikes,
Claiming it hosts the best parties with bikes.

The clouds play hide and seek all day,
Draping the sky in a playful way.
Nature's jesters with colors so bright,
Paint joy in the corners, sparking light.

So whirl with the vines, feel the fun vibe,
In this lush kingdom, where dreams subscribe.
For every truth holds a sprinkle of jest,
In the heart of the garden, feel truly blessed.

Hidden Depths of the Arbor

In the garden, hidden foes,
Whispers dance where nobody goes.
Roots entangle our tangled fates,
Gossip spreads like leaves on slates.

Lurking critters play their part,
Mischief brewing; it's an art.
Boredom hides beneath the bark,
Squirrels plotting in the dark.

Roses blush when secrets bloom,
Buzzing bees sing in the gloom.
What's that rustle? Who's to blame?
Is it the roots, or just the game?

Lost in laughter, we embrace,
Nature's quirks, a wild chase.
Among the leaves, we twist and twine,
Jokes sprout up like vines of wine.

A Tangle of Time

Time wobbles like a jelly dream,
Leaves tickle clocks that softly scream.
Bugs become the jesters here,
Telling tales to make us cheer.

Branches sway, a dance divine,
Frogs croak rhythms, oh so fine.
Clock hands jump like playful sprites,
Moments caught in leafy bites.

Here we munch on forgotten rhymes,
Calendar's soaked in fruit and limes.
Nothing matters, just the jest,
In this tangle, we're the best.

Sundials giggle in the sun,
Every hour brings more fun.
Time will twist, but here we stay,
In this garden, come what may.

The Garden of Unspoken Words

Whispers linger in the air,
Petals blush, oh, do they care?
Silence blooms in shades of green,
Butterflies know what I mean.

Words take root, yet dare not speak,
A shy breeze makes the roses squeak.
Voices hide beneath the stones,
Giggling like a pack of clones.

Every leaf, a hopeful sigh,
As birds chirp out a giggly cry.
Conversations veiled in shade,
Mysteries that won't all fade.

The garden thrives on laughter's thread,
Ticklish vines above our head.
Echoes of fun cling ever near,
In this place, the heart is clear.

Canopy of Secrets

Underneath this leafy dome,
Lies a world that feels like home.
Giggles bounce from branch to branch,
In this forest, we'll take our chance.

Caterpillars hold council tight,
Debating what's both wrong and right.
Their fuzzy suits are quite a sight,
Plotting mischief day and night.

Oaks drop puns like falling acorns,
Twisting phrases, breaking norms.
Look! A squirrel dons a crown,
In this kingdom, there's no frown.

Sunlight plays with shadows bright,
Secrets dance, oh, what a sight.
We're entwined, both small and grand,
In this canopy; life's unplanned.

Echoes Amongst the Green

In the garden where whispers play,
The leaves gossip through the day.
One says, "Did you hear that sound?"
A squirrel laughing, quite profound.

Laughter bounces off the trees,
Tickled by the playful breeze.
A rabbit joins with hops and flips,
As butterflies dance, doing quips.

The flowers gossip, bright and loud,
Their secrets shared, they feel so proud.
A bee buzzes, a comedic sting,
He thinks he's king of everything!

So let us roam this leafy land,
With giggles and a playful band.
Each step, a bark, and every turn,
In this green realm, we laugh and learn.

The Poetry of Twisted Trunks

Amongst the twists and tangled vines,
Stand trees with tales and silly signs.
One says, "I once danced in the rain!"
And then proclaimed, "But felt no pain!"

The branches sway, with quirky flair,
Creating shadows everywhere.
A fox joins in, with paws so light,
He breaks out into a funny flight.

Mossy hats on squirrels' heads,
Each strut a story, as humor spreads.
They trumpet laughs with each small hop,
In the woods, they can't quite stop!

So join the dance of trunks so bold,
Where nature's laughter never grows old.
In this vast land, with joy we mingle,
With jokes that even the trees will jingle.

In the Shade of Whispers

Beneath the leaves, where shadows twirl,
The whispers weave in a playful swirl.
A ladybug winks, sharing a dream,
While crickets chirp, creating a theme.

"Have you met the frog with a crown?"
He quips, "He hops with a royal frown!"
The sunbeams laugh, tickling the ground,
As mushrooms giggle without a sound.

In the shade, the laughter flows,
As friendship blooms where sunshine glows.
A wise old owl winks from his nook,
Telling jokes from a well-worn book.

Oh, let us gather, sip tea with glee,
In this secret spot, just you and me.
With nature's humor, we'll dance and sway,
In the shade of whispers, we'll laugh away.

Journeys Rooted in Green

On a path where the wild things roam,
The journey starts, it feels like home.
With each step, something humorous stirs,
As nature smiles and giggles purrs.

A snail on a quest, so slow yet spry,
Says, "I'll reach the end—oh, my, oh my!"
A butterfly drifts, with a wink so sly,
"Come join my race, let's reach for the sky!"

Lush grass tickles toes so bold,
Each turn reveals surprises untold.
With every turn, mishaps combined,
The giggles linger, fun intertwined.

So let's wander through this vibrant scene,
With roots entwined in shades of green.
A playful journey, laughter our guide,
In nature's arms, we'll joyfully glide.

Whispers of the Climbing Vine

A vine once dreamed of being tall,
But tripped on roots and started to fall.
It stretched and crawled with all its might,
And danced with the moon all through the night.

The squirrels laughed from branches high,
As the vine would twist then wave goodbye.
It sought the sun, but found a hat,
Now it's a fashion star—imagine that!

With every twist it told a joke,
While peeking from behind a oak.
"I'm not just green, I'm full of grace!"
A plant with swagger in its place.

Laughter echoed, leaves would sway,
As vines would prance both night and day.
In this garden of giggles and glee,
The climbing vine danced wild and free.

Secrets Beneath the Green

Beneath the leaves, a critter chats,
Tales of mischief from the cats.
Peeking out, it tells a tale,
Of how they slid down the old, damp rail.

A ladybug, pinning regrets,
Shared secrets of solitary pets.
Worms wiggled with laughter so bold,
As they twisted stories of treasure untold.

Who knew the lilies had such flair?
With petals soft, they started a dare.
To tickle the feet of strolling folks,
And giggle at all the funny blokes.

In the shadows where laughter gleams,
Life's little creatures spin their dreams.
A riot of whispers, a hidden scene,
In the garden lush, all bright and green.

Echoes of a Twisted Path

On a path that's never straight,
A snail emerged, it called it fate.
With a hat too big, it took a stroll,
Dreaming of becoming a rock 'n' roll.

A beetle joined, playing the drum,
While the flowers near began to hum.
With every beat, the path would sway,
Turning the garden into a ballet.

The hedgehogs snickered as they trotted by,
On their way to see the butterfly.
But slipped on petals, oh what a sight,
Rolling and tumbling into the night.

Echoes of laughter filled the air,
As whimsy bloomed without a care.
Each step forward, a giggle released,
On this twisted path, joy never ceased.

A Wreath of Shadows

In the twilight, shadows play,
Mischief creeps as night turns gray.
A wreath of leaves upon the ground,
Hiding secrets, all around.

The moonlight cast a glowing grin,
As crickets started their nightly din.
A cozy nook where whispers swell,
Unravel tales they cannot tell.

Toadstools twirled in a crazy dance,
While the wind gave them a chance.
"Come join the fun!" a firefly winked,
And the pumpkins around blinked and linked.

A wreath of shadows, laughter grows,
In the hush where magic flows.
Under the stars, all roam and play,
Amidst the quirks of night's ballet.

Paths of Nature's Melody

In the garden where the plants do prance,
A daisy told a rose to dance.
With every twirl, the petals blare,
While ants in tuxes waltz in air.

The tulips giggle at the sun,
As bees in bowties have their fun.
A sunflower spins in dizzy glee,
And whispers secrets to the bee.

Grasshoppers strum their tiny strings,
While ladybugs mimic opera kings.
The trees all sway, they take their turn,
For nature's stage, we all will yearn.

So join the beat, don't be a bore,
With petals bright, let's sing some more!
In this amusing floral spree,
Every bloom's a jubilee!

A Tale of Unraveling Vines

In a jungle thick, where mischief blooms,
A vine once plotted its famous dooms.
It tied the feet of a hopping frog,
And gave a snort to an old, wise hog.

Oh, the chaos of leafy disasters,
As lizards giggled, they were the masters.
A snake unwound, seeking a snack,
But stumbled upon a vine's tricky track.

The monkey swings with nimble grace,
But hit a vine—a real quick race!
He swung too far, flew past the tree,
Shouting, "Oh, wait! Come back to me!"

The jungle roared with hearty laughter,
All for a vine's silly disaster.
Nature's japes, oh what a find,
With wriggling roots and vines entwined!

The Unfurling of Dreams

In the morning light, the petals wake,
With dreams of sweetness, make no mistake.
Petunias plot to steal the scene,
While violets throw a pillow fight routine.

Buds burst open, dressed in delight,
As daffodils hop in airy flight.
Swaying alongside the morning dew,
Each bloom a dream, with skies so blue.

Oh lilies hum their treble sound,
While ferns make waves, all right and proud.
The cactus knits a pointy towel,
And smiles wide with a prickly growl.

With laughter shared in fragrant air,
The flowers breathe without a care.
In this garden of silly schemes,
Lies the tale of unfurling dreams!

Secrets of the Underground

Beneath the ground where no one peeks,
The worms devise their sneaky streaks.
They giggle as they dig all day,
While moles plan parties, come what may.

A rabbit hops with secret maps,
To uncover all the underground traps.
But instead of snacks, he found a show,
With burrowing critters putting on a glow.

The fungi dance in muted cheer,
While roots intertwine with tales to share.
"Got a mushroom hat?" the gopher sighs,
"Let's host a ball, I'll wear a prize!"

The whispers swirl 'neath the leafy shroud,
As laughter rises from the crowd.
In this world where few would roam,
The secrets thrive; it's their true home!

Possibilities Among the Twists

In a garden where secrets abound,
Plants gossip softly, making no sound.
Leaves wink at me with a playful tease,
While I ponder life amidst buzzing bees.

Tangles and turns in every direction,
Nature's maze calls for my keen detection.
I trip on roots, but laugh it away,
Where shadows dance in the light of day.

Vines grow higher, reaching for skies,
As I weave through laughter, ignoring the sighs.
Each corner turned brings a new surprise,
With every twist, more fun does arise.

The flowers smile, all dressed in their best,
With a playful spirit that never has rest.
Who knew a stroll could bring such delight?
In this lush playground, everything feels right.

Lush Paradigms of Enclosure

Behind the fence, where wild things roam,
A jungle of joy, a botanical home.
Cacti joke about hugging too tight,
While I dodge thorns in a foolish flight.

Ferns whisper secrets from ages long past,
Their leafy laughter leaves me aghast.
Photosynthesis parties after dark,
Inviting all critters to happily spark.

The smells of earth twist in playful air,
Flowers play dress-up without any care.
Among the foliage, the fairies cheer,
As I trip on my shoelace, well, that's my beer.

Each nook and cranny holds stories untold,
Of blooms in winter and greens made of gold.
With every glance, a new pun unfolds,
In this whimsical world, let the fun take hold!

Hidden Paths We Walk

Through tangled trails where I often stray,
Adventure awaits in a curious way.
Bumbling onwards, my compass awry,
With giggles from daisies as I pass by.

Mud on my shoes and leaves on my head,
Nature encourages me to misread.
Squirrels point fingers at my clumsy feet,
While trees look on with amused heartbeat.

From hidden alcoves, the critters await,
Their clever antics seal my fate.
With every misstep, the laughter grows,
In this wild maze where anything goes.

I find a hopping frog playing a tune,
A boisterous backdrop under the moon.
Every twist and turn brings its own quirky flair,
While I wander through this botanical fair!

Reminders of Botanist's Lore

With tweezers in hand, the botanists laugh,
Studying plants like they're writing a memoir draft.
Root systems tangled, they plot and they scheme,
Drawing maps of gardens in the wildest dream.

A cactus debates with a dandelion,
Who is the quirkiest of them in line?
As I join the chatter, the sun starts to fade,
In this riot of flora, my worries are swayed.

Petals that whisper while pollen takes flight,
Every sprout sharing wisdom in nature's spotlight.
Their tales are like riddles in jumbled array,
Each bloom, a funny memoir that brightens my day.

So here I wander, in realms green and bright,
With giggles from herbs that take off in flight.
In this botanical drama, I take my part,
With a smile that echoes from nature's great heart.

Secrets in the Soil

Digging deep, what a sight,
Worms in party hats, oh what a fright!
Roots are tangled, like folks on a dance,
Secrets whispered, given the chance.

Beneath the dirt, where socks go missing,
A treasure trove, oh, isn't it blissing?
Gnomes have parties when we're not near,
Juggling acorns, oh what a cheer!

In the muck, a story unfolds,
A saga of sprouts, if only retold.
Poking fingers, you might just find,
A talking plant that's slightly unkind!

So next time you plant, just tread with care,
For secrets and shenanigans fill the air.
With every seed, there's laughter to sow,
In the hidden world, where fun always grows.

The Enchantment of Green Walls

Climbing high, they weave their tales,
Poking noses through window gales.
Painted whispers, such a chat,
My green wall knows where the fun's at!

Old bricks chuckle, can't hold their glee,
As ivy tickles, swear it's just me!
Every vine has its own little prank,
Wrapping around, like a green-colored tank!

Tell me, dear wall, what's your trick?
How to make a dull day tick?
You say just smile and let life entwine,
Share your laughter, and you will shine!

A sprinkle of joy, some leafy fun,
In every twist, there's laughter spun.
So raise a glass to those green sprawl,
Keep it light; let the good times enthrall!

Tales of Timeworn Trellises

Oh, the tales those old beams could tell,
Of lovesick plants that bloomed so well.
Once a trellis, now in dismay,
Hipster vines trying to find their way!

Time has weathered, they creak and groan,
But oh, the gossip they proudly own!
Roses flirting with hopeful dreams,
While peas make puns and share their schemes!

Twists and turns in the afternoon sun,
Chasing butterflies, oh what fun!
Those wooden frames, a laughing spree,
Holding the weight of botanical glee!

So if you pass by, just have a seat,
Let the stories flow, oh so sweet.
For even old wood has dreams to chase,
In the dance of plants, there's a merry place!

A Symphony of Nature's Grasp

Listen close, the leaves conspire,
With melodies that never tire.
Nature's orchestra, full of cheer,
Sings of mischief, oh so clear!

Frogs drum beats on lily pads,
While crickets play the jolly lads.
Bees buzz sweetly, a buzzing choir,
In this garden, there's never a shyer!

The sun's the maestro, with beams so bright,
Creating shadows that dance at night.
And if you tune your ear just right,
You'll hear the frolic in the twilight!

So join the fun, let laughter soar,
In nature's grasp, there's always more.
With each new tune, let cheer abound,
As life in the garden spins round and round!

Nature's Silent Conversations

In the forest, leaves exchange jokes,
While squirrels prepare their finest hoaxes.
A bird sings a tale of lost bread crumbs,
As the bees buzz along, making hums.

Grasshoppers debate the best jumping tricks,
While ants march on with their heavy bricks.
The flowers chuckle, swaying with glee,
As the wind whispers secrets, just like me.

A raccoon plays peek-a-boo with a tree,
While frogs croak a tune, so carefree.
The sun winks down, with a playful glow,
As the world spins on, in a comedic show.

Nature's a stage, with laughter so vast,
Every creature's a player, having a blast.
So next time you wander, stop, take a pause,
And join in the fun of these wild applause.

Reflections in a Dewdrop

A dewdrop clings to a leaf so tight,
It holds reflections of morning light.
Here's a squirrel, with a nut on his chin,
Grinning at shadows, let the antics begin!

The sun tickles flowers, they giggle and sway,
While a snail glides by, taking all day.
A reflection of ants, all marching in sync,
In their tiny parade, who needs to think?

A butterfly flutters in a comical trance,
Wobbling around in a dizzy dance.
That dewdrop's a stage for moments so spry,
Where laughter runs freely, oh me, oh my!

In nature's mirror, the dawn starts to hum,
Who knew such reflections could be so fun?
So capture these moments before they flee,
For laughter and light, set your spirit free!

Stories Clinging to Bark

Trees hold secrets in their sturdy embrace,
Tales of a squirrel who won a quick race.
A woodpecker's rhythm creates a great beat,
While a rabbit munches on a leftover treat.

"Remember that time you lost your last nut?"
The oak chuckles loud, giving a gentle strut.
"Oh please," whispers elm, "Don't bring that up!
I still can't believe you thought you could jump!"

Vines twist around, they whisper and giggle,
As a beetle performs a hilarious wiggle.
Each ring on the trunk has laughter imbued,
In a world that thrives on joy, not on feud.

So next time you stroll where the tall trees grow,
Listen for laughter, let your heart glow.
For in the tall timber, the fun never ends,
Just stories of life, and the laughs that it sends.

Tangles of Tomorrow's Fruit

In the orchard, fruit hangs low and round,
Calling young critters, come gather 'round!
An apple on a branch, wedged in tight,
Complains, "Why do pears always pick a fight?"

Grapes giggle softly, from their tangled vine,
"Let's not be sour," they say, "We'll be fine!"
The peaches blush under the summer sun,
While lemons pout, not seeing the fun.

Rabbits hop by, their baskets in tow,
"Let's gather some joy from this fruity show!"
"Just watch out for bees; they'll steal your sweet bite!"
In the chaos of harvest, laughter feels right.

So gather your fruit and your laughter too,
In the tangle of life, find the funny view.
For tomorrow's joy is where we will pick,
Moments of silly, like a ripe, juicy trick.

Song of the Green Sanctuary

In a garden where whispers play,
The plants gossip in a leafy ballet.
Laughter blooms in each petal's grin,
While squirrels crack jokes, wearing a grin.

Potted plants tell tales so tall,
Of adventures where they had a ball.
They stretch their leaves for a sunny kiss,
Claiming victory in nature's bliss.

Butterflies waltz in colorful flocks,
While rabbits pull pranks in fluffy socks.
Frogs join in with a comedic croak,
As flowers giggle, it's all no joke.

In this sanctuary, fun's not a myth,
With every vine, there's more to sift.
So join the party, come take a look,
In this green haven, just open a nook.

Where Shadows Dance with Light

In the twilight, shadows waddle and sway,
Doing a jig in a playful ballet.
The moon chuckles, casting its beams,
While critters plot in whimsical dreams.

Lizards breakdance on the sun-warmed stone,
While owls crack wise in their twilight throne.
The starlit giggles tickle the night,
As shadows and light frolic in flight.

Bats zoom by with a fluttering shout,
Startling squirrels who leap about.
Fireflies giggle, twinkling like stars,
While the forest hums along with guitars.

In the space where darkness and brightness meet,
Every creature can't help but tap their feet.
So come join the shenanigans bright,
Where shadows and laughter banish the night.

The Tangle of Endless Growth

In a jungle gym of green and brown,
Every vine plays tag, never wears a frown.
Creepers climb high, waving to bees,
While fungi giggle on the warm, damp breeze.

A twist and a turn, a leafy embrace,
Nature's chaos, a fun, wild race.
Tangled roots tell stories untold,
Of playful days in the sun's warm hold.

Bramble bushes poke and tease,
While dandelions dance with the breeze.
Mischief blooms in every bend,
In this green hideout where hours extend.

With laughter growing on each winding path,
Nature's humor is a riotous math.
So venture within, take off your shoes,
In this tangle of fun, you'll never lose.

Veins of the Earth's Heart

In the soil where secrets intertwine,
Roots plot mischief in every line.
Earthworms chuckle, sewing a tale,
While ladybugs giggle without fail.

The heartbeat of soil pulses with cheer,
Bubbling giggles that only we hear.
Tiny critters race in a comedic chase,
While daisies hold court in their bright lace.

Every drop of rain is a splash of fun,
Sprouting laughter from everyone.
As mushrooms pop up with a playful grin,
The earth's jovial spirit draws us all in.

So listen close to the thump and the bump,
A merry rhythm, nature's sweet thump.
In these veins of green, life sways and sings,
In the heart of the earth, joy spreads its wings.

The Dance of Nature's Fingers

In the breeze, leaves wiggle and sway,
A merry jig on a sunny day,
Butterflies twirl with grace divine,
While ants march by in a conga line.

Clouds above gossip and play,
Sprinkling sunshine in a playful way,
Flowers blush in colors bright,
As daisies do the funky light.

Grasshoppers hop in a fancy gown,
While crickets chirp in made-up towns,
Nature's stage, a lively show,
With giggles echoing below.

So come and join this jolly spree,
In nature's dance, just be carefree,
With roots and wings, let's prance and spin,
In this wild place where fun begins.

Roots of Unseen Realities

Beneath the ground, roots are at play,
Whispering secrets come what may,
They tie their shoes and roll in mud,
Creating chaos, just like a flood.

With twirls and twists, they interlace,
In a rooty realm, we find our grace,
While mushrooms pop and giggle with glee,
Telling tales of the world that's free.

Worms wearing hats join in the fun,
Chasing the shadows under the sun,
They plan a party down in the soil,
Where laughter erupts and no one toils.

So dig deep down, unleash the cheer,
In unseen realms, where friends draw near,
A raucous gathering of roots and more,
Life's weird and wonderful underground score.

Whispers of Climbing Vines

Vines climb high, with a gentle twist,
Whispering secrets you can't resist,
They tickle the rafters, they shimmy and sway,
"Let's have a party!" they happily say.

With leafy hats, they sway and swing,
Charmers of summer, they dance and cling,
They peek through windows, play hide and seek,
Messy and fun, they're never meek.

Bouncing off fences, they laugh and cheer,
With a splash of green, bringing good cheer,
Each tendril a friend, in playful delight,
In the moon's glow, they twinkle at night.

So come on outside, let's join the fun,
Where plants are cheeky, and life's never done,
With climbing vines, we'll laugh and sing,
In their wild world, there's endless bling.

Secrets Entwined in Green

In tangles of green, secrets reside,
Hidden and waiting where few would abide,
Giggling gnomes in the thicket play,
In their leafy world, they dance all day.

A squirrel in shades gives a wink and a nod,
While bushes gossip of all things odd,
They whisper tales of the sunlight's glow,
Filling the air with a magical flow.

Frogs croak sonnets from lily pad thrones,
Plotting their antics with grumpy old stones,
Nature's conspiracies sprout and unfold,
In a laughing mosaic both silly and bold.

So wander these paths, through green and gold,
Where secrets weave stories yet untold,
With every step in this jungle scene,
You'll find the delights of the ever-green.

Shadows Beneath the Canopy

In a garden where squirrels plot,
Little gnomes sneak and laugh a lot.
A rabbit with a top hat asks,
If you see his friend in silly masks.

The leaves whisper tales of late-night fun,
Where shadows dance under the glowing sun.
A butterfly pranks with a sneaky win,
As frogs play piano with a grand, loud grin.

In corners where sunlight dares to peep,
Funny creatures join in a merry leap.
Each vine a talent, each shoe a size,
They burst in laughter beneath bright skies.

So, if you wander beneath this green,
Spy these antics you've never seen.
For in this realm where odd meets glee,
The garden's secret is joy, carefree.

Echoes of Celestial Leaves

From branches high, a joke takes flight,
Whispers of leaves in the cool moonlight.
A crow caws loud at a bushy tale,
While a lizard chillin' hits the nail.

Stars gather round for a laughter spree,
As acorns drop like comedy.
A raccoon, dressed up for a show,
Steals bananas—just to steal the glow!

Mice in shades slide down the vine,
A game of tag, it's simply divine.
Twirling in shadows, they weave a rhyme,
A melody crafted in perfect time.

So raise your cups filled with morning dew,
To the mischief brewed by the playful crew.
Where echoes of giggles float in the breeze,
There's magic spun through the rustling leaves.

The Lattice of Dreams

A trellis tangled in knots anew,
Where kites dance wildly, just like the dew.
Daisies laugh as daisies grow,
While unseen giggles spread joy below.

A snail in slippers glides along,
Chasing the rhythm of a silly song.
While shadow frogs play leapfrog proud,
Cheering on lilies, gathering a crowd.

Each tendril twists with a witty tease,
Planting hope in a flower's sneeze.
The laughter rings through sun-kissed air,
As sprites prance by without a care.

So swing by this whimsical embrace,
Find humor rooted in every space.
For filling hearts with endless beams,
Is the magic held in this lattice of dreams.

Where Tendrils Embrace the Sky

Weaving whispers, tall vines conspire,
To tickle clouds that float higher.
A squirrel in a cape takes off and flies,
Overwhelmed by laughter, he nearly cries.

Each shadow grins with a playful jest,
Awaiting the sun's daily fest.
While owls pretend to read the news,
Advising turtles on their best shoes.

The breeze chuckles as it jumps about,
Swaying the tendrils, there's no doubt.
In this chaos where giggles collide,
Wonders and whimsy take a wild ride.

So come, dear friends, join in the cheer,
Where laughter echoes for all to hear.
In this delightful twist of spine,
Tendrils entwine, and all will be fine.

Gaze into the Green Abyss

In the garden of giggles, where greens take a leap,
Laughter blooms wildly, secrets to keep.
A hedgehog with goggles, I've heard it's a sight,
Sipping on dew, oh what a delight!

The daisies are dancing, the sun's in a haze,
Worms wear top hats, in their wormy gaze.
A squirrel with acorns, conducting a band,
Sings silly sweet tunes, it's all quite unplanned!

Behind every bush, a joke waits to sprout,
In this wacky green world, who knows what's about?
With giggles aplenty, the leaves twist and shout,
Gaze into the green, let your worries flout!

So come join the fun, let your cares drift away,
In this leafy maze, it's a wild, funny play.
Where every odd creature has something to share,
Dive into the green, if you dare, if you dare!

A Whispering Grove of Time

In a grove where whispers tickle the ears,
Trees tell tall tales of laughter and cheers.
An oak with a bowtie, so dapper and spry,
Swears he's a tree who can twirl and fly!

The wind carries giggles from leaf to leaf,
While mushrooms gossip in hilarious grief.
A fox in a vest keeps watch from a stump,
He's judging the critters who dance like a chump!

With shadows that giggle and sunlight that winks,
Every step leads to waddles and shrieks.
Tickling the trunks, the vines swirl around,
In this grove of time, the silly is found!

So come heed the whispers, feel time bend and sway,
With laughter like rain, let's enjoy the day!
Amongst this green chorus, life's easier, see?
In a grove where the silly is always set free!

When Leaves Speak of Love

Oh, the leaves are a-flutter, with secrets to share,
　Whispering sweet nothings, floating in air.
　A dandelion sighs, "I've got quite the crush!"
On a charming green bud, in a soft, breezy hush.

They blush in bright colors, a leaf's romance,
　Falling for petals in a whimsical dance.
　A ladybug swoons, in her polka-dot dress,
　Declaring her love with a little bug mess!

In a riot of colors, they twirl through the breeze,
　Flirting and laughing, with every in-breeze.
　A sparrow sings silly, as he flits from a vine,
Saying, "Love is a riddle, but oh, it's divine!"

So next time you wander 'neath branches above,
　Listen for laughter, and whispers of love.
Amongst the bright leaves, where whimsies ensue,
　Even nature is giddy, with tales just for you!

Under the Cloak of Nature

Beneath the green cover, mischief unfolds,
With critters in costumes, daring and bold.
A raccoon in pajamas is stealing a snack,
While owls play charades, with a theatrical quack!

The shadows are giggling, as twigs start to bend,
Nature's a jester, with laughter to send.
A hedgehog in slippers, with dance moves so sly,
Spins round and round, oh my, oh my!

While mushrooms wear crowns, it's a royal affair,
Hosting a banquet, with parties to spare.
With giggles and glee, the critters declare,
Life's under the cloak, where fun makes us dare!

So come join the revels, where the wild things roam,
In this capricious kingdom, we all find our home.
With laughter as armor, and joy as our song,
Under nature's great cloak, we truly belong!

The Rise of Tender Roots

In the garden, sprouts do wiggle,
They plot their rise with every giggle.
A tiny leaf, a daring sprout,
Says, "Watch me grow, there's no doubt!"

With sun on face and rain in shoes,
They dance in dirt, they chase the blues.
Worms find them funny, try to poke,
While grass rolls eyes and cracks a joke.

A ladybug flies in with flair,
"You tiny greens, do y'all need air?"
They puff their chests and yell, "We're cool!"
As breezes play in the leafy school.

Roots stretch wide in their grand quest,
Who knew they'd have so much fun, no rest?
In their leafy world of giggles and glee,
They toast with dew — a giggly spree!

Portraits of Verdant Whispers

Among the leaves, secrets glide,
As stems exchange tales side by side.
A whisper of wind, a rustle here,
Leaves burst with laughter, oh what a cheer!

A beetle says, "I'm quite the catch!"
"Don't be silly, you're just a patch!"
They giggle and tickle, a grand parade,
In shades of green, mischief is made.

The daisies sway, with grins so bright,
Tiptoeing close to the moonlit night.
"I once knew a shrub, a clumsy guy,
He tripped on a root and kissed the sky!"

With petals unfurling, each tale unfolds,
In laughter's embrace, the garden holds.
So come and listen, beneath the light,
Where whispers of green create pure delight!

Delicate Threads of Twilight

As dusk descends, the vines entwine,
They weave goodnight tales, all in line.
With giggling stars and crickets' song,
They sway together, where they belong.

The moon peeks in with a quirky grin,
Spilling silver laughter, inviting the din.
"Tell me, dear petals, what's the fuss?"
"The roses think they're the best of us!"

The glowworms giggle, teasing the leaves,
"Hey there, tall stalks, don't you take reprieves!"
With knots of charm and charms of knots,
They share their antics, tying in thoughts.

As shadows dance on the garden floor,
Each blossom breaths secrets to explore.
Delicate threads in twilight bound,
In whimsical tales, joy is found!

The Canopy's Mysteries

Hidden up high, where the branches meet,
The canopy giggles, a playful retreat.
With critters peeking from cozy nook,
"Guess what? I spied on the ground folks' look!"

A squirrel shimmies, his acorn stash,
"Why do humans run? They're such a bash!"
From the leafy heights, they tell with glee,
"Let's toss some leaves and make them squeak!"

The ancient oaks, wise with their years,
Share secrets of laughter, of joy, and of tears.
"Watch that bird, she's quite the flier,
Once mistook a hat for a nest to retire!"

With breezy whispers, mischief takes flight,
In the canopy's heart, it's pure delight.
So join the laughter, never be shy,
In the tree's warm embrace, let your spirit fly!

Twists of Fate in Twining Growth

In a garden where vines dance high,
A squirrel once tried to give it a try.
He slipped on a leaf, what a sight!
Now he claims he can fly with delight.

A chatty bird perched right above,
Said, "Listen up, I'm a leafy dove!"
With a wink and a squawk she did tease,
"Growth can be tricky, take care, if you please."

Two tendrils met in a curious twist,
Planning a party, none could resist.
But their decorations got caught in the breeze,
"Who knew Ivy could throw such a tease?"

Yet in their folly, they laughed with glee,
Turning their blunders to pure jubilee.
Life's twists may tangle, but hold on tight,
For laughter is found where plants take flight.

Beneath the Green Veil

Under leaves where shadows play,
Lies a secret plan for the day.
With whispers and giggles, oh what a crew,
Plotting mischief with a hint of dew.

A rabbit joins with her quick little paws,
Crafting a caper that deserves applause.
"Let's swap our hats," she declared with a grin,
"Wearing ivy will surely bring us a win!"

As they donned their leafy attire,
Their laughter grew ever higher.
A turtle strolled by, quite confused,
Said, "What's this fashion? I'm totally amused!"

Beneath the green veil of playful delight,
They frolicked 'til stars twinkled in sight.
In this garden where whimsy prevails,
Every moment sings, beneath those green trails.

Tales of the Evergreen Path

In a thicket where tales come alive,
The critters all gather with dreams to contrive.
A hedgehog spun stories of bravery and might,
While a snail scoffed, "You're quite a sight!"

With a twig for a mic, he hitched a ride,
On a passing breeze, he laughed with pride.
"What's faster than me? I hear you will ask!"
"A rumor," he said, "I'm too slow for that task!"

Meanwhile, a fox with a cunning grin,
Offered a riddle on the joy within.
"What grows without legs, yet wanders around?
I'm ivy, my friend, in growth that astounds!"

So the tales spun deeper, with laughter and glee,
Each creature with quirks, a delightful spree.
In whispers of green, where all paths intertwine,
The evergreen stories, quite wonderfully twine.

Climbing toward Solstice

As golden rays peeked through the trees,
Two vines decided to catch a breeze.
"Let's reach for the sun, it's time for a climb!"
But tangled they got, oh what a rhyme!

A frog on a leaf called out with a cheer,
"Keep up the spirit, no need for fear!"
With optimism grand, they rolled with the falls,
"We'll laugh at our troubles, the sun always calls!"

So, they hopped and they twirled in their leafy mess,
Swearing by laughter, they'd never transgress.
With every slip and every new twist,
Their journey was riches that none could resist!

As day turned to dusk, ivy waved and swayed,
They climbed toward the sky, unafraid and unfrayed.
With each joyful leap, they approached the solstice,
And danced in the glow, what a wild bliss!

Veils of Nature's Reverie

Leaves whisper secrets with a grin,
A squirrel juggles while birds sing in.
Rabbits in shades of emerald jest,
Trees eavesdrop, they know the best.

Laughter rustles in the air,
Nature's chuckle, a wild affair.
Breezes play tag with a dandelion,
Who knew green could be so fine?

Mushrooms sport hats, quite absurd,
Joking about this and that word.
The sun winks down from its throne,
In this antics-filled forest, we're never alone.

Amidst blooms and vivid dance,
A ladybug spins in a trance.
In nature's romp, we find delight,
As vines weave stories in the light.

The Unseen Beneath the Surface

In the garden, a gopher's grin,
Digging tunnels, where to begin?
He bumps a worm, their eyes wide,
"Mud pies," says the worm, "Come, let's slide!"

Rats in hats hold a soirée,
With mushrooms dancing in disarray.
Fungi gossip, spread the news,
While beetles don fancy shoes.

A raccoon's caught in a hat theft,
Stumbling on plants—oh, what a mess left!
Under the soil, a party ensued,
As earthworms provided the food.

Shadows stretching with a giggle,
Roots intertwining, they don't wiggle.
Nature's playful, always a tease,
Watch out for fun—it's sure to squeeze!

Chronicles of a Green Heart

A vine in a tangle, quite in a twist,
"Come, take a look!" it calls, heartily missed.
A cactus sings ballads to a bee,
"Your buzz is the sweetest, dance with me!"

Petals gossip, their colors so bright,
Who wore it better? Give me a fright!
The gardener stumbles over a hoe,
Plants chuckle softly; they know the show.

Lily pads float with a wink and a nod,
Inviting frogs to a dance once they prod.
Moths in tuxedos flap and sway,
In the moonlight, they make a fine display.

Grapevines twist, narrating their lore,
Sipping cool dew, wanting more.
In this garden of mirth and cheer,
Green hearts beat loudly, there's nothing to fear!

A Labyrinth of Lushness

In a maze of green, hedges scheme,
A turtle pauses, lost in a dream.
"Which way is up?" he ponders with grace,
While fireflies flash like stars in this place.

Vines entwine in a playful chase,
With daisies giggling, they win the race.
Snakes slither softly with wit and charm,
Giving a shout, "No need for alarm!"

A hedgehog dressed for a garden ball,
Hoping a lady will come to call.
Pansies whisper with snickers so sweet,
As rabbits hop to the drum's lively beat.

Through this tangle, joy's come alive,
In the jungle where the playful thrive.
Nature's oddities, wild and spry,
In the labyrinth, we laugh, oh my!

The Language of Climbing Hearts

In a garden filled with sneaky vines,
They whisper sweet nothings in tangled lines.
Each leaf a giggle, each branch a joke,
Climbing higher, oh, how they poke!

Laughter sprouts from roots below,
As friends do tumble in joyful throe.
Their jokes get stuck, much like their shoes,
In this leafy dance, who can refuse?

Twists and turns lead to laughter's glee,
Like a grapevine cup of tea, oh me!
Petals chuckle, petals sigh,
What's this, a diary up in the sky?

When hearts entwine, they start to sway,
Telling tales in a funny way.
Listen close, and you'll soon find,
Climbing hearts leave no one behind!

Harvesting Dreams from the Walls

On walls so sturdy, dreams hang tight,
Plucking wishes in broad daylight.
With baskets made from woven cheer,
Collecting giggles, year after year.

Some dreams are tiny, some take a leap,
Like squirrels who gather and never sleep.
One's a wish that's rather tall,
"I hope that cat won't make that call!"

We giggle as we snip the greens,
Harvesting hopes from leafy scenes.
Mismatched socks and silly schemes,
Tumble from our climbing dreams.

So pick a dream, it's ripe and bright,
A cherry laughter, pure delight!
With every strum of our heart's tune,
We dance beneath the silly moon.

Remnants of Forgotten Tales

In the shadows of vines where stories lurk,
Ghosts of laughter in every quirk.
Forgotten fables stuck in the green,
Who knew the secrets lie in between?

A frog in a suit tells a silly chase,
As owls wear glasses, proud in their place.
The tales get tangled like spaghetti strands,
In a world where whimsy always stands.

With every twist, the laughter grows,
At the edges of crooked rows.
Old chairs and socks from days gone by,
Start to giggle, oh me, oh my!

With remnants of tales upon each leaf,
We gather snippets beyond belief.
In the labyrinth of vines, we find,
A treasure of chuckles intertwined!

Reflections on Woven Vines

Reflected laughter in a leafy mirror,
Woven dreams make our spirits clearer.
With every curl, each twist and turn,
We learn the secrets our hearts discern.

A vine swings high, a squirrel takes flight,
Bouncing on hopes, oh what a sight!
Knots and loops in a merry dance,
Who wouldn't join this leafy romance?

With mirrored smiles and silly grins,
The laughter bubbles, the fun begins.
Giggling shadows dance on the grass,
We stick together, none shall pass!

Each vine a whisper, each leaf a shout,
In this glorious chaos, there's never a doubt.
So let's reflect, let's weave our rhyme,
With laughter and dreams that stand the test of time!

Secrets in the Shade

In the garden where whispers dwell,
Worms hold secrets, so do the snails.
Ivy giggles in the sunlight bright,
Dancing shadows bring delight.

A creeping vine with a curious grin,
Hiding truths of how it began.
A garden party just for plants,
They've all dressed up, oh what a dance!

Bees tell tales of flowers' charms,
While daisies and dandelions share their alarms.
Joking roots trip one another,
Silly vines tease their leafy sister.

In this shade, laughter grows wild,
Each petal's giggle is sweet and mild.
Secrets bloom with a mischievous air,
In the garden of jests, we find joy rare.

Trellis of Hope and Memory

On the trellis where dreams entwine,
Old stories climb and twist in line.
Laughter echoes through leafy loops,
As memories spin like playful groups.

There once was a vine with a knack for talk,
It shared all the gossip while taking a walk.
With roots deep set in the past it grew,
Claiming each tale as if brand new.

The sun peeks in with a wink and grin,
And leaves on the trellis join in the din.
Each petal a punchline with stories to sell,
A comedy club where all grow well!

With a twist of the stem and a chuckle of grass,
The garden of joy is a vibrant class.
Here every vine wears a cap and a gown,
In this playful plot, there's never a frown.

Chasing After Sunlight

Chasing rays while the dew drops play,
Vines do giggles by the light of day.
A wobbly leaf in the morning mist,
Jumps for joy, can't be dismissed!

Squirrels join in with a playful prank,
While shadows dance on the old farm tank.
Every sunny beam is a chance to tease,
As petals rustle with the gentle breeze.

Rabbits hop while ivy sways,
In a merry chase, they spend their days.
Each sunlit spot a treasure of fun,
Where all of nature laughs as one.

They race and tumble, a wild delight,
Under the cover of warm daylight.
Chasing shadows, the laughter grows,
In this garden, joy forever glows.

Leaves of Yesterday

Underneath the big oak tree,
Old leaves gossip, can you hear me?
They chuckle over who's fallen down,
And how many wore that muddy crown!

Each crinkle tells a tale untold,
Of sunny days and nights so bold.
With whispers soft and laughter light,
They reminisce about their flight.

The breeze brings jokes from seasons past,
As leaves recall how long they've lasted.
In this confab of shadows and sun,
The tales keep spinning, never done!

Leaves of yesterday wear jokes like hats,
Swapping quips with the cheeky sprats.
In this arena of fun and games,
Nature's comedy never wanes!

Through Gnarled Branches

In a tangle of vines, I lost my shoe,
Beneath a green curtain, the squirrels all flew.
They chuckled and chattered, with acorn in tow,
While I practiced my dance moves, in mud down below.

A raccoon peeked in, with a look of surprise,
I waved at him gladly, he just rolled his eyes.
The branches above seemed to giggle and sway,
As I stumbled and fumbled, oh what a display!

The tree trunks were grinning, with knots in their bark,
I swear I heard laughter, as I tripped in the dark.
A fairy emerged with a wink and a grin,
She pointed at me saying, "Let the fun begin!"

With gnarled branches close, I embraced the absurd,
Nature's own comedy, so silly, so blurred.
I danced through the chaos, a joyful parade,
In a world full of laughter, my worries then swayed.

In the Heart of the Garden

Among the bright blooms, I took a short stroll,
Where bees wore tiny goggles and cartwheeled with soul.

A cabbage patch prince wore an oversized crown,
The daisies were giggling as they twirled 'round town.

A worm in a tux, he boogied all night,
Claiming veggies needed a dance that was tight.
The carrots did salsa while the roses went slow,
Even radishes joined in, putting on quite a show!

A drumming beetle joined in with a bang,
While the moon kept on shining, the garden it sang.
There's humor in petals and chaos in scents,
Where greens share their jokes with absolute intents.

I laughed at the scene in this Eden of glee,
Where hilarity blooms, living wild and carefree.
With tendrils of laughter, my heart felt so light,
As flowers danced merrily well into the night.

Where Shadows Meet the Light

Where shadows meet light, the laughter is bold,
A butterfly bumbles, its charm quite untold.
It zigzags and flutters, in search of a mate,
While crickets compose tunes, it's sure sounds of fate.

A shadowy cat, with a grin carved in glee,
Watched bugs share their gossip, not caring for me.
The sunbeams they danced, igniting the air,
While frogs played the banjo, without any care.

A ladybug joined, with her polka dot dress,
She twirled with a wink, in a playful mess.
Oh, the chortles and chuckles, the critters all gave,
In this quirky hideaway, where laughter can rave!

As dusk painted hues, the fun intertwined,
In this charming tableau, all joyfully blind.
So next time you wander, remember this plight,
Where shadows are dancing, and laughter feels right.

A Tapestry of Leaves

In the rustling trees, where secrets unite,
A tapestry glimmers, with colors so bright.
The leaves held a meeting, each sharing a laugh,
As gusts of sweet wind devised a new craft.

With oak saying, "Hey, join our leaf-swinging game!"
While birch rolled her eyes, "You're always the same!"
A gust gave a chuckle, uproariously bold,
And retold the tale of the tree that was old.

Each leaf wore a story, a tale intertwined,
Of raindrops and sunshine, to life they were blind.
They giggled and jostled, a merry brigade,
In this leafy cabaret, a dance serenade.

As dusk settled softly, and shadows took flight,
The leaves shared their secrets, all tender and light.
In a tapestry woven with humor and cheer,
They whispered of joy, their season sincere.

Serpents of Green in the Dusk

In the garden at twilight, they wiggle and sway,
Chasing shadows like kids who just want to play.
Their laughter's a whisper, the night's gentle tease,
As they sneak up on daisies, not caring for bees.

With a flick of their tails, they twirl in delight,
Beneath the soft glow of the firefly light.
They search for the snails, a fast-snacking race,
And tell silly tales, all while struck by grace.

A snake made of vines, in deep emerald hue,
Pretends he's a cowboy, with boots made of dew.
He rides on a worm, a wild rodeo,
While crickets applaud with a curious show.

As the night takes a bow, they laugh 'til they cry,
The joy of the dusk, where the comedians fly.
In each rustling branch, hear the secrets they share,
In this funny world, there's magic everywhere.

The Universe in a Leaf

Under a leaf, the stars seem to dance,
A tiny cosmos caught in nature's romance.
With ants as astronauts, and bugs that delight,
They zoom through the veins, to the edge of the night.

A ladybug pilot, with goggles so round,
Races her buddies, through the lost and found.
With laughter so loud, it's a giggle brigade,
As they soar past the dewdrops, in their leafy parade.

The moon hangs above, a giant's rich cake,
But the critters just munch on the crumbs they can take.
It's a feast fit for kings, served on green velvet,
With a side dish of humor that none can forget.

In this little galaxy, so charming and bright,
Every whispering breeze carries echoes of light.
Where laughter is currency and joy takes the lead,
In the universe of leaf, all hearts will be freed.

Carving Dreams in the Green

In a world made of greens, where mischief runs wild,
The grass thinks it's clever, playing tricks like a child.
With blades that can tickle, and roots that can dance,
They scheme for a moment, a comical chance.

A gnome with a grin sits atop a sweet sprout,
With a hat filled with dreams, he's spinning about.
The flowers keep giggling at their silly play,
While bunnies join in for a hop and a sway.

Fog rolls in soft, like a blanket of yawn,
Where phantoms of fun greet the shimmering dawn.
They sketch little props in the dirt with a twist,
Finding joy in the mundane, they simply can't resist.

Each hour a new giggle, each moment a jest,
Carving dreams from the green, oh, it's simply the best!
In the realm of the plants, where humor ignites,
Life's a whimsical journey of laugh-filled delights.

Ghosts Among the Tendrils

In the vines that entwine, a ghost party brews,
With fluttering skirts, and shimmering hues.
They float with the ferns, and tickle the grass,
Sipping on moonlight, letting good times amass.

A waltz with a whimsy, they shiver and shake,
While the mushrooms are giggling, for goodness' sake!
These spirits of laughter play peek behind leaves,
As they plot their mischief—oh, as one believes!

With roots as their friends, and tendrils around,
They hear every secret the earth has to sound.
And when dawn starts to break, with joy in their hearts,
They vanish like whispers, yet never depart.

So, next time you wander in gardens so green,
And feel a soft breeze, where you've never been,
Remember the ghosts who play games in the vines,
For humor and fun are what nature defines.

www.ingramcontent.com/pod-product-compliance
Lightning Source LLC
Chambersburg PA
CBHW072223070526
44585CB00015B/1471